DOORS

TO THE REAL

YOU!

DOORS

TO THE REAL

YOU!

Deborah Elum

Copyright © 2015 by Deborah Elum

All rights reserved. No part of this book may be reproduced or transmitted in any form or by any means, electronic or mechanical, including photocopying, recording or by any information storage and retrieval system, without written permission from Deborah Elum.

Printed in the United States of America

For information, contact:
All That Productions, Inc.™
P.O. Box 1594
Humble, Texas 77347-1594

All Scripture quotations, unless otherwise indicated, are taken from the King James Version Copyright © 1990 by Thomas Nelson, Inc. Used by permission.

ISBN: 978-0-9903422-3-6

ACKNOWLEDGMENTS

I thank my God and Father; Jesus, the Lover of my Soul; and Holy Spirit, my Teacher for inspiring me to write this book. God, You are truly my source.

I would like to thank my husband, Randy, who always encourages me to pursue the purpose and destiny for my life. To my son, Brian, who always supports and helps me with my book projects.

Thank you to my pastors, Roy and Ann Chapman, a man and woman, after God's own heart. To my mother, Lucy Peterson, who took me to the house of the Lord at a young age. To my aunt, Patricia Briscoe who lead me and my sister, Joyce to the Lord. To Evangelist Billy Graham who taught me about the Lord Jesus Christ.

To my friends in the ministry Debra Starr, Evangelist Nancy Clement, and Prophetess Debe Campbell. Women who blaze for God!

TABLE OF CONTENTS

Introduction   1
Everybody Has a Purpose

Chapter One   7
Behind Closed Doors

Chapter Two   13
Doors to the Eyes

Chapter Three   21
Doors to the Mouth

Chapter Four   29
Doors to the Ears

Chapter Five   37
Doors to the Heart

Chapter Six   41
Designed for Purpose and Destiny

"For I know the plans I have for you," declares the L ord, "plans to prosper you and not to harm you, plans to give you hope and a future."

Jeremiah 29:11 NIV

Introduction

EVERYBODY HAS A PURPOSE

One night, I had a vision from God. In the vision, I saw hundreds of grey doors. Some of the doors were large and some were small. Each door was sitting on top of a mound of dirt. What was God trying to tell me? What was He trying to reveal to me?

Then, I saw Jesus standing behind a large white door. He was full of power and glory. As the door opened, beams of radiant light burst forth and shined from all around the door. It was a troubling night vision yet, interesting at the same time.

One day, the Holy Spirit spoke clearly to me. He said that many people had many wonderful dreams in them. But because of what they had let in through the door of their inner man (the real person inside), their gifts and talents were locked away. What He had called them to do was hidden behind a door that would never be opened. They would never fulfill their true destiny because of what they allowed to hinder them (pride, procrastination, doubt, fear, unforgiveness, etc). Those very things caused their purpose to remain buried. The white door represented the people who were walking in the plan and purpose for their lives.

God never begins anything without a plan or vision to finish it. Luke 14:28 says that, "For which of you intending to build a tower, sitteth not down first, and counteth the cost, whether he have sufficient to finish it?" Ecclesiastes 1:9 says that, "The thing that has been, it is that which shall be; and that which is done is that which shall be done." That is why God knows how everything is going to come out. He designed it, built it, and finished it. All we are doing is walking out what God has already done.

In the book of Jeremiah, God is talking to Jeremiah about why He created him. In Jeremiah 1:5, God was very clear that Jeremiah was created for a specific purpose. Before he was in the belly of his mother, God told him that he was created to be a prophet to the nations. Then, He told him that even before the foundation of the world, he was in His plans. In other words, Jeremiah was predestined before the world ever existed.

God has predestined all of us. He has called us before the foundation of the world. Interestingly enough, everyone and everything has a reason why they exist. For example, the purpose of a door is to provide an entry or exit. Doors come in different colors, shapes, sizes, and materials. They are created for different looks, functions, and purposes. A metal door provides more protection than a glass door. However, a glass door provides a clear view of what is going on inside and outside. But no matter how large or small doors are, the same purpose applies; to keep something in, keep something out, let something in, or let something out.

Introduction: Everybody has a Purpose

I wrote this book to encourage you to let your desires and dreams shine forth through the doors to the real you! Ask God to unlock your gifts and talents that they may be used for His purpose to fulfill your destiny.

Introduction: Everybody Has a Purpose

Prayer for Purpose

Father,

Thank You for unlocking all my gifts and talents that are within me. I am grateful that as I walk in my purpose and destiny for my life, others are being blessed by what You have placed within me. Thank you that I live a life pleasing to You, in the victorious name of Jesus, Amen.

For nothing is secret, that shall not be made manifest; neither any thing hid, that shall not be known and come abroad.

Luke 8:17

1
Behind Closed Doors

We are made up of three parts; body, soul, and spirit. We are not a body that has a spirit and soul. We are a spirit that has a soul and lives in a body. The soul or inner man consists of the mind, will, intellect, and emotions. Ever since God created man, He has been trying to get us to get this, the body or flesh should be controlled or moved by the Spirit of God.

What is going on behind closed doors? What is really going on inside? Well, it all depends on you. Your body is governed by which one is the strongest, the spirit or the soul. The one you feed the most will be the strongest.

Think of it this way, your body is like a computer. It will do what it is programmed to do. The body is designed to manifest good or evil. If you download the Word of God with confessions, meditations, and prayers, you will respond the way God designed you to function.

However, sin in the body is like a virus or like infected software to a computer. It will cause the computer to malfunction. It might not stop working all at once. Sometimes it is a slow process. Sometimes one virus gives access to let other viruses in. Eventually, it causes the computer to stop accessing vital information or even steal important information.

Sin is the same way. It stops you from accessing who God created you to be. It will start to destroy or erase important information and it can even shut you down so that you are completely useless. How does the right information get into your spirit you ask? God is a Spirit and He communicates with your spirit. Your spirit then communicates with your soul (inner man), and your inner man communicates that information to your body. This is how the flow should be.

Too often it is only the soul that feeds the body. The soul is built up or torn down by what it hears, sees, feels, and speaks. What you see, hear, and speak is important. You must be diligent in reading, mediating, and confessing God's Word in the Holy Bible. This is also a must; you must hear the preached or taught Word from an anointed person of God. That does not mean we cannot learn from what others speak but if you want your life to be what God has desired, you need to hear the Word of God from someone who has a right relationship with God.

Our body was created with doors so that we can get the right information into our spirit that causes our inner man to become strong. In other words, whatever is going on behind closed doors will eventually be revealed or manifested openly. It will be seen in our actions, heard in our conversations, and noticed in our responses. God has created an awesome physical and spiritual body for you. Then, He equipped it with doors to the real you. The physical and spiritual doors are your ears, mouth, eyes, and heart.

Mark the Door With Protection

God instructed Moses to mark all the doorposts of their houses with the blood of a lamb to keep something out, His judgment. God was about to pour out a judgment upon the Egyptians. God wanted to keep something out. He wanted to keep out or protect His people from the judgment that the firstborn male would die.

²¹Then Moses called for all the elders of Israel, and said unto them, Draw out and take you a lamb according to your families, and kill the passover.

²² And ye shall take a bunch of hyssop, and dip it in the blood that is in the bason, and strike the lintel and the two side posts with the blood that is in the bason; and none of you shall go out at the door of his house until the morning.

²³For the LORD will pass through to smite the Egyptians; and when he seeth the blood upon the lintel, and on the two side posts, the LORD will pass over the door, and will not suffer the destroyer to come in unto your houses to smite you.

²⁴And ye shall observe this thing for an ordinance to thee and to thy sons for ever.

Exodus 12:21-24

As the death angel traveled freely throughout Egypt to carry out the sentence, he would enter into each house where he did not see the blood on the door. As the angel came to the door of an Israelite, if he saw the blood on the door, he could not enter.

²⁸And the children of Israel went away, and did as the LORD had commanded Moses and Aaron, so did they.

²⁹And it came to pass, that at midnight the LORD smote all the firstborn in the land of Egypt, from the firstborn of Pharaoh that sat on his throne unto the firstborn of the captive that was in the dungeon; and all the firstborn of cattle.

³⁰And Pharaoh rose up in the night, he, and all his servants, and all the Egyptians; and there was a great cry in Egypt; for there was not a house where there was not one dead.

Exodus 12:28-30

The death angel came to destroy anyone or any animal that was not behind the door that was covered with the blood. Not one family, servant, or animal was exempt unless the blood was applied to their doorpost. Can you imagine the power the death angel saw coming from that door? The blood of the Lamb represented the blood of the real Lamb, Jesus. The door represented Jesus and the blood represented His power to protect and deliver. Only life (not death) could enter in. In John 10:9, Jesus said, "I am the door: by me if any man enter in, he shall be saved." Jesus was, is, and will always be the "Door of Life."

Prayer for Behind Closed Doors

Father,

Thank You that You protect and deliver me from anyone who tries to set a snare or trap for my life. Deliver me from anything that would pull me off of the divine and wonderful destiny that You, Father God, have for my life. I choose to abide in the Secret Place where You feed, guide, and protect me. I will not stray from Your precepts or Your commandments, in the name of Jesus, Amen.

The light of the body is the eye: therefore when thine eye is single, thy whole body also is full of light...

Luke 11:34

2
Doors to the Eyes

When I was about four years old, my father drove our family from Texas to Oklahoma for a family reunion. Just seeing the blue skies and mountains with snow-covered peaks was a wonderful and breathtaking experience for me.

It is very interesting to me how the eyes can see. Just think about how the eyes can see color, shapes, sizes, objects, people, nature, and animals. To be able to experience the wonders that God has created. To see His wonderful creation is an honor we sometimes take for granted.

Since we are God's creation, how should we see ourselves? He does not want us to see ourselves as defeated, sick, or broken. We should see ourselves as finishers, winners, and overcomers. We should see ourselves as the blessed and victorious people of God. God sees us in our finished state. He sees us victorious with nothing missing and lacking in our lives. God sees us as strong finishers. Declare that you are one of them. Amen!

Only when you realize who you really are in Christ can you walk in complete victory, power, and dominion. Take another look in the mirror. Not just the mirror on your wall but into the mirror of the Word. In Deuteronomy 28:13, God says that He shall make us the head, and not the tail; and we shall be above only, and not beneath. Take hold of the promises of God. See yourself as a winner.

Our eyes were meant to behold only what is good, lovely, or of a good report. But in this present day and time, we are also exposed to things that are not good, lovely, and of a good report. What happened? We must first revisit the book of Genesis.

Heaven is Filled with God's Glory

The first man and woman walked in the supernatural realm, the realm of glory. A realm where everything was full of peace, joy, love, prosperity, and rest. Where the glory of God was present and everything was "sweatless."

They could see things with their spiritual eyes. God brought His very presence in their midst. Adam and the woman were clothed with the glory or in the manifested presence of God. That same glory was in the Garden of Eden.

Then in Genesis, the Bible records a conversation between the first woman and a cunning and tricky serpent.

> [1] Now the serpent was more crafty than any of the wild animals the LORD God had made. He said to the woman, "Did God really say, `You must not eat from any tree in the garden'?"

> ²The woman said to the serpent, "We may eat fruit from the trees in the garden,
>
> ³ but God did say, 'You must not eat fruit from the tree that is in the middle of the garden, and you must not touch it, or you will die.'"
>
> ⁴ "You will not surely die," the serpent said to the woman.
>
> ⁵ "For God knows that when you eat of it your eyes will be opened, and you will be like God, knowing good and evil."
>
> ⁶ When the woman saw that the fruit of the tree was good for food and pleasing to the eye, and also desirable for gaining wisdom, she took some and ate it. She also gave some to her husband, who was with her, and he ate it.
>
> **Genesis 3:1-6 NIV**

God did not tell the woman that she could not touch the fruit. What God told her is recorded in Genesis 2:16-17.

> ¹⁶And the LORD God commanded the man, saying, Of every tree of the garden thou mayest freely eat:
>
> ¹⁷But of the tree of the knowledge of good and evil, thou shalt not eat of it: for in the day that thou eatest thereof thou shalt surely die.

So God said that if she "eat of it" she would die. So the woman did not tell the truth. How is it that she could be deceived before even partaking of the fruit from the tree? Because she had already eaten of the fruit in her heart. Here are important principles of how sin enters into the body and the destructive force it causes if it is not stopped.

> [14] But every man is tempted, when he is drawn away of his own lust, and enticed.
>
> [15] Then when lust hath conceived, it bringeth forth sin: and sin, when it is finished, bringeth forth death.
>
> **James 1:14-15**

> [16] For all that is in the world, the lust of the flesh, and the lust of the eyes, and the pride of life, is not of the Father, but is of the world.
>
> **1 John 2:16**

Something in the Natural Released Something in the Supernatural

When their eyes were opened, it was obvious that a major spiritual event occurred. Immediately, their eyes were opened to experience evil for the first time in their existence. It affected everything they saw. It affected everything they knew and who they were. Where everything they experienced was once glorious, now entered; pain, lowliness, betrayal, denial, sadness, fear, hate, and everything that was wicked.

Then, the eyes of both of them were opened, and they realized they were naked; so they sewed fig leaves together and made coverings for themselves (Genesis 3:7 NIV).

Adam never criticized, complained or murmured against God or any of His creations before the fall. He saw the good in everything and in the Woman. He was too busy doing what God had created him for. He was living out his purpose.

When the doors of Adam's and the Woman's eyes were opened, they were very disappointed at what they saw. It was not what they expected at all. Where they once saw each other as pleasant to look at, now, they were ashamed of themselves. They felt ashamed to look at each other. Something that they did in the natural changed something in the spiritual realm (1 Corinthians 15:46). He felt ashamed for the first time as he looked at his wife.

Closing the Natural Doors and Opening the Spiritual Doors

When they ate of the fruit, they were saying that they desired to see with the natural eyes more than the spiritual eyes. They did not realize it until it was too late that they opened the natural doors and closed the spiritual ones.

Get this truth in your spirit right now that God is not a man, that He should lie. Neither is He the son of man, that He should repent. "Whatever He said, and shall He not do it? Or hath He spoken, and shall He not make it good," (Numbers 23:19).

You can believe that whatever God says shall come to pass. You do your part and God will do His. We have to do things in the natural realm to change things in the spiritual realm. What is your part? Your part is that you have to close the natural doors and open the supernatural ones.

In other words, do not look at what you see. Look at that which will be. The first step is to repent of unbelief. Then, you must call into being things that were not as though they were (Romans 4:17). You have to open your mouth and call your body whole and well. Call your bank account full. Call your marriage restored. Call your child or children walking in their destiny and purpose. Call your family blessed and saved. Call yourself walking in high favor.

As you speak and believe, faith increases and the spirit of faith will manifest what you have been speaking. Thank God that He gives you vision, wisdom, knowledge, understanding, and the plans to accomplish what He promised all by faith.

Don't Push Past God

Next, you have to have patience. God is the Master Builder and Strategist. He knows the timing, the finances, and the people you need to help you. You do not want anything out of season because it will be destructive to you and the people around you. Do not allow yourself to push past God. That means, do not get ahead of what God is doing in your life.

You have to learn to be content where you are as the promises of God manifest in your life. Then, whatever God says to do, do that. God usually starts you off with the small things first. Start where you are. Do not try to win the world first. Start where you are with the resources you have available. Saint Luke says it this way, "He (that's you) that is faithful in the little is faithful in much..." (Luke 16:10).

Prayer for Doors to the Eyes

God,

I anoint my eyes afresh to see my life seated with You in heavenly places. My eyes will look unto the hills from which cometh my help. My help comes from You, Lord. My eyes choose to focus on godly things, in the glorious name of Jesus, Amen.

Set a guard, O Lord, before my mouth; keep watch at the door of my lips.

Psalm 141:3

3
Doors to the Mouth

The lips are the doors to our mouth. Our mouths speak our thoughts, feelings, and opinions. Did you know that if you could see in the spiritual realm your words would look like containers? A container holds or carries something. What does it hold? Well, your words hold the power of faith to produce what you say. It is like receiving a package in the mail. There is something inside for your use.

Once words are spoken either God's angelic or the devil's demonic forces take those words and go to work on producing what you said. Psalms 103:20, states, "Bless the Lord, ye his angels, that excel in strength, that do his commandments, hearkening unto the voice of his word." The angels are swift to carry out the Word of God. Another key to destiny is to hear God's Word and obey.

What force do you want working for you? Life or death? With our words, we speak either life or we speak death. Words of life justify us and make the divine things of God come to pass in our lives. But, words of death condemn or pronounce us guilty. Remember, every word we speak is important because they carry the force to create or destroy.

³⁶But I say unto you, That every idle word that men shall speak, they shall give account thereof in the day of judgment.

³⁷ For by thy words thou shalt be justified, and by thy words thou shalt be condemned.

Matthew 12:36-37

God designed us to use His Words to change lives and to speak a word in due season to those that are weary. By confessing His words, we speak our destiny into the earth realm. We declare; as it is in heaven, so let it be on the earth!

God provided the materials (His Word), the tools, and the plans (our destiny and purpose). He even provided the wisdom, knowledge, and understanding on how to build it. All He needs is faithful laborers with mouths that speak uncontaminated words.

I love what the Bible said about Jesus, He only spoke what He heard the Father say (John 8:28, John 5:30). He saw then He spoke it into existence. He always got what He spoke. He saw things like they were in heaven. He looked into the spiritual realm of heaven and pulled them down to the earth by the power of the spoken Word.

Don't Leave the Door Unlocked

When a house is being constructed the builder chooses the plans, materials, and tools necessary to complete the project. The foundation is poured then a frame is constructed (Psalm 103:14), the outer shell then the inside. The bottom is assembled then the top. Before the house is completed, doors are added to protect the valuable contents of what is being built and installed inside.

When God made you, He also chose the plans, materials, labor, and tools necessary for the real you to function as designed. Then, He handed you the keys for you to "manage it." When God drew up the plans for you, you were created to be a wonderful house, an exquisite show place. Let us go inside the real you.

Whatever you have been letting out of the door of your lips is in you, it is the real you. Your innermost being has been meditating on what you speak, hear, and see. When you receive something as truth and you keep listening to it over and over again, it will eventually become the truth to you.

Matthew 12:24 says, "...for out of the abundance of the heart the mouth speaketh." In Hebrews 11:3 it says that, "Through faith we understand that the worlds were framed by the word of God, so that things which are seen were not made of things which do appear."

What power! God wants us to operate in that way. The words in God's mouth are filled with power. In the book of Genesis, the Word of God tells us that He created worlds just by speaking them into existence. In the first chapter of Genesis, God saw everything He said. He spoke light into the darkness and it came to pass. Then, He named what He created.

[1] In the beginning God created the heaven and the earth.

[2] And the earth was without form, and void; and darkness was upon the face of the deep.

And the Spirit of God moved upon the face of the waters.

³ And God said, Let there be light: and there was light.

⁴ And God saw the light, that it was good: and God divided the light from the darkness.

⁵ And God called the light Day, and the darkness he called Night. And the evening and the morning were the first day.

Genesis 1:1-5

As God continues to reveal Himself to us, we move from faith to faith and glory to glory. As we too understand the power of our words, we should guard the door.

Don't Let the Devil "Back Door Ya"

We frame our world by the words we speak. We have to speak the words of God to see godly results. God's words contain His promises to you.

We must not be snared with the words of our mouth and taken with the words of our mouth (Proverbs 6:2). If something is snared it leads you into a place or situation from which escape is difficult. In other words, the wrong words leave an opportunity for the devil to use them against you. In the book of Ecclesiastes, the Word of God talks about paying attention to when to speak and when not to speak.

A time to rend, and a time to sew; a time to keep silence, and a time to speak;

Ecclesiastes 3:7

One of my friends would say, "Don't let the Devil Back Door Ya," by confessing ungodly things about yourself. Do not give him access to you to come up from behind and hit you with something you did not see coming.

I have heard people say that their children are driving them crazy, how the bills are killing them, or how old they feel. It is leaving the door wide open for the enemy to come on in and take from them. It is an open invitation for a thief to take advantage of them.

In Proverbs 18:20 the Scripture tells you that you will be satisfied with what you have been speaking.

> [20] A man's belly shall be satisfied with the fruit of his mouth; and with the increase of his lips shall he be filled.

The Bible is full of the Wisdom of God. It instructs us on what to say and what not to say. In Joel 3:10, "Let the weak say I am strong." Let the weak confess what they want to see manifested or to see come to pass. You do not deny the condition exists but you deny it the right to stay there. Do not keep rehearsing the condition, speak to it and tell it to go!

Do Not Criticize, Complain, or Murmur

The language of speech is an awesome gift from God. To speak, we have to open the door of our lips. That is why the lips are the last opportunity to stop the wrong thing from exiting from our hearts through our mouths, and into the atmosphere. It is the last checkpoint before words of life or death exit for a destination.

¹³ The wicked is snared by the transgression of his lips: but the just shall come out of trouble.

¹⁴A man shall be satisfied with good by the fruit of his mouth: and the recompence of a man's hands shall be rendered unto him.

Proverbs 12:13-14

Prayer for the Doors to the Mouth

God,

Set a guard over my mouth and keep watch over the door of my lips. Give me the wisdom on when to speak and when to keep silent. Let my words be pleasing unto You, in the name of the Holy One, Jesus, Amen.

Then he openeth the ears of men, and sealeth their instruction.

Job 33:16

4
Doors to the Ears

How would you feel if you heard a knock on your door? To your surprise, it is the garbage collectors. All of a sudden, they started bringing trash cans into your living room. Then, one of them says with a smile, "We want to share this stuff with you," and they begin dumping it out in your living room. How would you feel?

You are a worthy vessel not a trash can. The Lord wants to protect us in every way. A talebearer or gossiper is like trash collectors. They collect mess and trash and dump it where it does not belong. Remember, you are not a trash can where people can empty their garbage into your life.

So do not give a talebearer or gossiper a key to the door because they will open it wide. Talebearers cause strife between people. Keep the door locked from these types of people. The Lord wants us to protect every door including our ears. Gossip has the same effect as a wound does to the body.

> [20] Where no wood is, there the fire goeth out: so where there is no talebearer, the strife ceaseth.

²¹As coals are to burning coals, and wood to fire; so is a contentious man to kindle strife.

²²The words of a talebearer are as wounds, and they go down into the innermost parts of the belly.

²³Burning lips and a wicked heart are like a potsherd covered with silver dross.

²⁴He that hateth dissembleth with his lips, and layeth up deceit within him;

²⁵ When he speaketh fair, believe him not: for there are seven abominations in his heart.

Proverbs 26:20-25

The ears are designed to hear sounds. It is one of the ways we receive communication from people, animals, etc. It is interesting that the ears have a door that closes only with the assistance of the hands. In other words, the doors to the ears are normally opened 24 hours a day.

Sounds are consistently coming towards us. What we listen to most of the time is our choice. After that, we make a choice whether we will respond. People respond to what they feel is worth their time, energy, and effort. We put a value on it so we respond.

There have been many times when people expected me to respond to a question or a comment. I have learned that if I do not value it, I simply choose not to respond. I do not open the door to them. Why? Because I am learning to listen for certain sounds, sounds that will bring more of God to my life. I am listening for a people that know how to speak words that have the sound of faith.

Faith Has a Sound

There is a sound to faith. Faith rides on the sound of God's Word. God is always talking. In John 1: 1, the Bible says that "In the beginning was the Word ..." That tells me that the Word (Jesus) was producing a sound, the Word was the sound of God. The sound of God is faith. So God cannot be separated from His Word (Jesus) or His Spirit (the Holy Ghost) for they are One.

As we open the doors of our spiritual ears and listen to the Word of God on a consistent basis, faith will increase. God wants each door to be fortified with power, force, and strength, so that anything that is not of Him will not prosper against us. Everyone has something to say. If they are not speaking what God is saying about the situation then, they are just talking words, words that are not just empty but, empty of God's power.

Words are Made Up of Sounds

You might have received a bad report from your doctor or received a bank notice that your bank account is overdrawn. Do not focus on what you are hearing with the natural ears. Cancel those reports and believe the report of the Lord that all is well no matter the report. Let the Word of God speak to your spirit and say you are blessed, your body is blessed, your marriage is blessed, your bank account is blessed, and even your business is blessed. Why? Faith always speaks because Faith has a voice. Faith talks back to you and says, "Listen up. In the natural it might seem that way but listen to what I am saying that will change the natural to the supernatural." The Spirit of Faith then manifests that faith in your life. Sometimes the Spirit of Faith (or the Holy Ghost) can speak through a person, through the Word of God, or directly to you. Let faith arise within you and let your enemies of doubt, disbelief, sickness, discontentment, and fear be scattered. In Exodus 3:7-10, God spoke these words to Moses:

> [7]And the LORD said, I have surely seen the affliction of my people which are in Egypt, and have heard their cry by reason of their taskmasters; for I know their sorrows;
>
> [8]And I am come down to deliver them out of the hand of the Egyptians, and to bring them up out of that land unto a good land and a large, unto a land flowing with milk and honey; unto the place of the Canaanites, and the Hittites, and the Amorites, and the Perizzites, and the Hivites, and the Jebusites.
>
> [9]Now therefore, behold, the cry of the children of Israel is come unto me: and I have also seen the oppression wherewith the Egyptians oppress them.
>
> [10]Come now therefore, and I will send thee unto Pharaoh, that thou mayest bring forth my people the children of Israel out of Egypt.

After God fulfilled the first promise that He would deliver them, He was now ready for them to walk into the promise of rest. He wanted to bring them to a land of rest and provision. In Numbers 13:31-33, God told Moses to send men from each tribe to spy out the land He had promised them.

> [31] But the men that went up with him said, We be not able to go up against the people; for they are stronger than we.
>
> [32] And they brought up an evil report of the land which they had searched unto the children of Israel, saying, The land, through which we have gone to search it, is a land that eateth up the inhabitants thereof; and all the people that we saw in it are men of a great stature.
>
> [33] And there we saw the giants, the sons of Anak, which come of the giants: and we were in our own sight as grasshoppers, and so we were in their sight.

When the spies returned, all but two of them (Joshua and Caleb) brought up an evil report. It was an evil report because they did not believe that God could help them prevail against their enemies. What the people heard in the natural was that they would not be able to step into the promises of God.

They only heard with their natural ears. They chose not to remember the report of the Lord that the land belonged to them.

God already knew His people would come up against enemies. He knew all the challenges they would face and the battles they would have to fight. But God was with them. They forgot that God is not a man, that He should lie; neither the son of man, that He should repent: hath He said, and shall he not do it? or hath he spoken, and shall he not make it good (Numbers 23:19)?

If God has made promises to you then rehearse them in your ears. Get them down in your spirit. Let the Word of God come alive in you. Refuse evil reports and move into the promise land for your life.

⁵The Lord GOD hath opened mine ear, and I was not rebellious, neither turned away back.

Isaiah 50:5

Prayer for the Doors to the Ears

Father God, the Creator of All Things,

You give understanding and wisdom. Thank you that you protect my ears from evil communications; from gossipers, from backbiters, and from those that speak out of envy or any other wrong speech. Thank you, that you anoint my ears afresh to hear Your voice, in the name of Jesus, Amen.

My mouth shall speak of wisdom; and the meditation of my heart shall be of understanding.

Psalm 49:3

5
Doors to the Heart

The heart is designed to bring nutrients, water, and oxygen to each cell of the body through the blood. It is the blood that takes away the waste from each cell. It takes away waste that is not needed or may be harmful to the body.

The heart is more than an organ that just pumps blood. When we understand that the natural heart is attached to the spiritual body, then that is key to understanding more about how they function together. When the natural heart holds onto things that are harmful or toxic, those same toxic things cross over into the spiritual heart. The spiritual heart although invisible to the naked eye is just as real as the natural heart.

> [35]A good man out of the good treasure of the heart bringeth forth good things: and an evil man out of the evil treasure bringeth forth evil things.
>
> **Matthew 12:35**

Words are Seeds

Words are seeds. God's Word is unique because His Word is the seed, the water, and the fertilizer. That is why you must continue to study and speak God's Word over and over. In Matthew 13:23 Jesus says, "But he that received seed into the good ground is he that heareth the word, and understandeth it; which also beareth fruit, and bringeth forth, some an hundredfold, some sixty, some thirty." The heart acts as the soil that grows what you mediate on. As you continue to speak it and meditate on it, understanding and revelation will come to your spirit. Then, you are able to speak and see results.

If you plant an orange tree you expect oranges. If you plant an apple tree eventually you will expect apples, right? Now, that all depends on the seed, soil, water, sunlight, and fertilizer it receives. So, if you are only getting a few oranges or none at all after years of taking care of a tree, you know that something is wrong.

The same is true in your life. Are you planting in your heart doubt, gossip, unforgiveness or fear? That is the reason why it is not producing a good harvest. If you are not watering it with the Word then that is why it is not producing. Are you covering up the "Son" from shining on it, with a cloud of guilt and shame? Well, that is why it is not producing.

Even in a properly maintained garden, weeds must still be pulled out. Remove the weeds of sin and a godly crop will spring up. Start speaking life and life will come. Matthew 12:34 says, "... For out of the abundance of the heart the mouth speaketh.

Prayer for the Doors to the Heart

Lord,

I anoint the doorpost of my heart with the blood of Jesus. Teach me to mediate on Your Word. Thank You that as Your Word is planted in my heart, an abundance of love, peace, joy, hope, finances, health, and goodness is springing forth, in the matchless name of Jesus, Amen.

I have declared the former things from the beginning; and they went forth out of my mouth, and I shewed them; I did them suddenly, and they came to pass.

Isaiah 48:3

6

Designed for Purpose and Destiny

When you are designed to do something, you just get a knowing on how to do it and you enjoy doing it. It will come easy for you. If you are designed to be in sales, you can sell just about anything. If you are designed to be a teacher, you can explain it so others can learn.

I remember years ago when I first started visiting my dentist. I knew that she enjoyed what they did. She looked forward to coming to work. As she examined each patient, she would hum a song. It was obvious that she was designed to be a dentist. She once told me, "I should be paying you to do what I do."

It was the same with the lady that owned a postal business in our neighborhood. She enjoyed what she did. It showed even in the staff that worked for her.

I am sure like most of us, both the dentist and the owner of the postal business experienced difficulties in their life. But what made the difference was they knew their purpose and did it!

In conclusion, do not settle for just existing while you are on this earth. Do what you were designed to do. Start right where you are. If you were designed to be a doctor, then go back to school. If you were designed to have a maid service, start cleaning. Start right where you are and God will help you find your way to your wonderful purpose and great destiny.

Prayer for Purpose and Destiny

Lord,

Thank You that You have given me an abundant life filled with love, peace, joy, wisdom, knowledge, and understanding.

Thank You that the plans You have for my life are so much greater than anything I can image, ask or think. I ask for wisdom and You are granting me the ability to do what You have called me to do. Thank You for directing me and strengthening me to complete every assignment for my life. Thank you that the thoughts You have about me are thoughts of continual peace, prosperity, and hope. You know my purpose. Thank You, Holy Spirit, that You lead, guide, and strengthen me to do what God has designed me to do. I never lack for ability, I never lack for opportunity, and I never lack for money.

Lord, You are meeting every need that I have physically, spiritually, emotionally, socially, and financially. My life is a satisfied life because of an Amazing God, in the name of Jesus Christ, Amen.

Scripture References

"For I know the plans I have for you," declares the LORD, "plans to prosper you and not to harm you, plans to give you hope and a future."

Jeremiah 29:11 NIV

For nothing is secret, that shall not be made manifest; neither any thing hid, that shall not be known and come abroad.

Luke 8:17

The light of the body is the eye: therefore when thine eye is single, thy whole body also is full of light...

Luke 11:34

Set a guard, O Lord, before my mouth; keep watch at the door of my lips.

Psalm 141:3

Then he openeth the ears of men, and sealeth their instruction.

Job 33:16

My mouth shall speak of wisdom; and the meditation of my heart shall be of understanding.

Psalm 49:3

I have declared the former things from the beginning; and they went forth out of my mouth, and I shewed them; I did them suddenly, and they came to pass.

Isaiah 48:3

Notes

Notes

Notes

Notes

www.ingramcontent.com/pod-product-compliance
Lightning Source LLC
Chambersburg PA
CBHW061254040426
42444CB00010B/2380